POOROETRY
Poems Better Left Unsaid

by TOM TYPINSKI

TOM TYPINSKI

DEDICATION

To the ones who said their stuff was not up to snuff. It is. Just let someone else feel it and you will soon find it resonate like a plucked guitar string. For the ones who think their thoughts don't matter, they do; they matter to you.

TOM TYPINSKI

CONTENTS

THERAPY 101

"Look into the face of a child
Measure how long you smiled
Before the mem'ry claimed
How long would children remain
How long could children remain" - ATHENA The Who

The newest habit of "non-addictive personalities"
Therapy: Where dream recall
meets past performance in an
outpouring of thought repressed
and feelings seized — suspended
in the belief that grief exists
to insure growth and the gross
errors of our parents' guidance
can be outgrown by examining
them firsthand with a stranger
who's willing to listen one hour
a week, until the insurance runs out.

In a cubicle like a tomb
or a room in your mind,
light sneaks in, trickles,
through Venetians blind to
the outside where your voice echoes
and her head bobs until you get
to the point of recognizing
"BREAKTHROUGH"
and life resumes like something
malignant has just been
removed.

But then you realize it's
"you"
You're the room
and the blinds
and the voices
"not to be taken away..."

Keep the dreams.
Leave the gloom.

STILL, LIFE

Two young lovers
taking pictures of each other.
Going places.
Playing games. Playing parts.
Playing with each others hearts
in the park. In the dark
where each movement left a mark.
They discovered with wordless action
sensations like spattering raindrops
touched with need and discovery
and the time that only memory can hold.
The stillness in their silences, the breath of life.

THE ENGLISH CLASS

The English Class
from first to last
was more or less
like passing gas.
Sometimes a fizzle
sometimes a blast.
Some drawn out
And then, some fast!
But all in all
The more that passed
The better we felt and
The more we laughed!

OPTIMISM - (I think that's how it's spelled):
The ability to keep your eyes high enough out of the shit you got
yourself into, to see what you can get into next.

STRAIGHT LINES across eyebrows, forehead to chin symmetry, lips of equal, sensual thickness, teeth as long as the nose is sloped, toes tanned and polished though too much space and too much bone, waist slenderly endless and flat hipped, pants sit like a denim smile arced under inny enough for a hand to slip in, thick wide mouth even sexy when eating, thin neck on a jawbone that curves like Sweden, set unhiding and uninhibited beneath sloe-gin eyes, better looking yet in glasses, rectangular pink-tinted, against angular cheekbones in straight attitude of "fuck off" via missionary position.

WE BOYS

Nothing a good girl likes better than a bad boy.
And we were one big group of bad, bad boys.
We cornered the market on badness, both in attitude and antics.
In sheer number we were an army, with 88% of us over 6 feet,
we were deadly — looking and acting. Girls had no chance.
And we didn't even dance.
Reputations tarnished with gentlemanly pretense.

JUST

LUST
IS WHAT IT IS
LUST
IS NOT A WOMAN
IT'S HER PARTS
LUST
IS LOVING A MOMENT
IN TOUCH, TASTE, SIN, SEX
LUST
IS NOT ENOUGH
TO GET YOU LAID

DR. JEKYL IN HIDING

So there's that yin/yang
    In the silence you can scream
that in/out of ebb/flow
    and no one seems to hear
tides pulling you to
    the night is crowded with
drink or not, to eat
    loneliness, the moon even
to excess, or not, too
    turning away, brilliantly
overdue – an over do – all
    proclaiming your foolishness
without remorse or regret
    sending you away in sober
to face the daze with
    suffering until the night
"devil may care – fuck it!"
    meets day.

BAD BREEDING

All nose and no chin
All forehead, no cheeks
All hips, no breasts
Bad breeding.
Bad posture,
Slouching attitude
Leaning toward forever
While walking past.
Better the smile crooked
and the teeth straight
Than the teeth crooked
and the smile great!

<u>CHURCH</u>

Long faces mumble through rote prayers said without intention.
These people are already dead
"Forgive, forgive, forgive"
Stand up, sit down fight, fight, fight.
"Lack, lack, lack" — yack, leave.

Every song is a death march
Every message is negative, guilt-filled.
I am floored by the ridiculous knowledge
that these people put themselves through
this torture week after week.
Eternal-suffering-forever-being-Catholic - Amen.

Pomp and pretension.
It reminds me of the Python skit
where the monks walk in a line and hit their heads with bibles.
"mumble, mumble"…forgotten rules.
The Church of the Lemmings,
"Follow me…
…off this cliff."
They stand to listen to a "reading"
they didn't get the first thousand times they heard it.
It's such a joke, even God is laughing.
What fools they must be!
All in uniform, identical, in a row, sharing the same scowl.
Just like last week, year, decade.
They never tell Jesus was a rebel,
that He really was different.
Just hit me with a stick and get it over with.

<u>**CHAMP (1986)**</u>

He stuck his nose out too far, too fast
And as the oncoming traffic passed
A car caught his snout and
he whirled about
in the dust of the highway island;

to whirl and bleed in the land
between the lanes
crying in the pain of a mouth
now a memory
and a tongue full of brain.

His face disgraceful
in its bloody nakedness
whirling in circles
from momentum and delirium

No one stopped nor consoled as
he rolled his last breath
in the dirty, dying grass.
He took a blind chance and
all I hear is his boy calling for him.

<u>POOROET</u>

There once was a boy from the city
Who spent all his time looking pretty
He wasted his life
He caused himself strife
by spending his life and not living.

<u>PREGNANT MAN (1986)</u>

All thoughts grow stories in my womb
Churning in my stomach
and in my chest until birthed,
when the pain gets too great
and emotions too deep.

I lose sleep, temper reigns and
with the fall of a snowflake I'm
brought to tears of joy and sympathy.

Many deformities lay coiled.
Not to spoil the beautiful child
that's patient yet diligent
brought by good health and bliss,
I kiss the creature goodbye,
to rest, to reform
in the closet of my chest.

And in one shining moment
in one glorious stream when
it seems nothing can stop it
the creation is released.
I cease work to wonder at
the marvel of its birth.

Is there a moment when the solace of emptiness
resounds within?

WORKING

Undisturbed.
Most people don't realize the value of solitude.
Most abuse it with television or bad news.

Embrace the quiet.
Embrace the dark.
It's there where everything is seen.
Soliloquy to poetry.
Emptiness to much.
See what hasn't yet been seen.
believe in it until
you can touch it
touch it like your dreams
on the black-felt velvet
of an Elvis portrait.
The day brings inspirations,
the night, memories.
The twilight, a mix of things,
only you can add for meaning.

CONSUMPTION

My Dad used to eat sugar
And chug milk
gulped tall glasses of water
And sipped beer

He could have drunk gasoline
and puked barbed wire
and I still would have admired him.

He was the one
who walked in front of me.
Somehow, I intrinsically knew this.
I knew I was somebody before I was me;
someone greater, that I strove toward.

<u>BELVEDERE</u>

Like the men in
endless succession,
climbing and descending,
walking up while falling down
on ladders,
steps,
ropes,
rails,
whatever it takes to get up,
get ahead,
get somewhere
in this optical illusion of life,
only to end as a still life
in a portrait of someone else's imagination.

*Return to dreams of golden leaves on sunset lakes
and days of peace*

BRAIN DUSTERS (1985)

The cabinetry and crevices of my medulla need sweeping.
Cobwebs and dustballs are collecting
in my cranium, from lack of use.
The ole Muse is on vacation
I need airing.
Everything's static
The paint's peeling and the rat population's doubled.
The lightbulbs need replacing.
My ideas come in streaks of one every other week.
I feel like the zoo custodian replaced my matter with hippo shit.
After being lit for so many years in a row,
the fire's quit, packed up, gone home.

Creativity is something which describes my shopping lists.
The dust is thick like a refrigerator guard grid.
It could choke a vacuum hose and bring a spider to fits.
It's not a nice place inside my head, not even to visit.
Kind of musty, like a mausoleum bed.
There's lots to shed before it shines
like the times of a younger man.
Embrace release.
That is my only chance.
Or else I'll end up with a hat full of sand.

Happy as a lark
in a park
while a dog barks

<u>MY BROTHER WARNED ME</u>

The Pall Mall lay smoldering in the grass
my heart beat faster
Dad didn't allow smoke in the house
yet his pipe was always smoldering
I had seconds
I was less than six
I looked up to him
and the red burning ember flared,
"here's your chance."
It was less than a digit on my small hand
it burned my lips and my fingertips
and all my nervousness tasted was fire.

His hand grabbed me and lifted me and turned me to him,
"If I ever catch you smoking I'll kick your ass"
My trembling legs and knobby knees
held me like Tinker Toys
as he dropped my body
from his 6 feet of heroism.

He died of emphysema at 67
but I never smoked again.

<u>THE FROST MADE ME THINK OF…</u>

other frost on other windows
winds whipping snow
a cold sparrow
nights I couldn't go
places I hold fond to know
black sky, white ground
no sound but the snow
feelings I never should've shown
many cold noses
patterned etchings on glass
that glow

<u>A DAY IN THE LIFE OF WHAT MIGHT HAVE BEEN</u>

The struggle is always trying
to try harder
and the harder everything comes
the more the struggle

Things just aren't working;
everything except me

So I must be the fight I must win
disposition is what I must conquer

My personality is slipping
I'm losing something within

The electric heat hurts my eyes
dried tears for
this self-induced stress is absurd

Anger doesn't work at anything
except to spread anger
A sweeping flame of harsh words
destroying in its wake all those
precious trusts it took so long to build

A day in the life of what might have been.

So, if you're a person who's
out of balance
would it help if your arms
were longer?

SPRINGTIME RINGS IN WARM THOUGHTS
ON COLD MORNINGS

On a crisp, cool spring morning
you wake to think of hot June
Sleeping without clothes or covers
Being with your lover
When twilight turns to moonlight
where the stars match their maker.

Thoughts of beaches with kids in the sand
and all the tan women
clad in your best imagination
all curves and fluorescent neon on black mats.

In a blink you're back
brought sober by the goosebumps on your shoulders
and the incessant meowing of the cat.

PUZZLE

So often you sit
a watchman for phrases
which might fit
together
pulling
cogent wholes of space
to reunions of severance
bits of matter that to the
untrained eye lie undiscovered

__THE PAINTER__

Poetry in your motions
striking unlikely impressions on canvas
Pollock directed 1999's Prince reflections
in inks and jewels
constructed like layered whirlwinds

The only way to catch the spirit
is to be the spirit
it takes practice
Like Tai Chi
Bodybuilding
Zen and the Art of Motorcycle Maintenance

Painting is the expression of the deep soul
There is passion in friction
Canvas to bristle
Paper to Pen
a potter's thumbs to clay
the wetness of the liquor cross your tongue.

I'm sorry Barry
but I can't get to the heart
of this matter
There is no heart in death
it must have been long and
it must have been painful

Your painting still hangs
in my office, "MFA"
the "Midnight Funk Association"
and I think of the poem I wrote
about it
it inspired me so.

About the blackness
and the cherry
and the blue cresting waves.
You appreciated that poem
You were astounded.
Because of that painting
we replaced woe.

"TURN TO THE LEFT..."

We have no friends who are fashion sensitive.
They rely on another's opinion,
a girl, a friend, a salesperson,
to dictate what they should wear to where.

None have the guts to expose a bust,
to let a calf show in public, or an ankle to ogle.
Too conservative, they rely on a fashion page or mannequin
and so resemble the same. They lack imagination.
To dress the mannequins
in silk and satin
body's contorted like reality,
mouth agape, maybe,
or in a pout, because to be
so droll one must not be
so stout as to look at life
with an everyday set face
a smile does not say it all-
though there is much to smile
about as a fashion doll
dressed in Saks best,
never unclad in store window,
never cold, uncaring when left alone.

The day's light changes but the
expressions don't
a spotlight adjusted like invisible sun
warming a space of plaster and cloth,
the only warmth on a mannequin's heart.

<u>REPRAY</u>

The tears on the window
like the rain on my face
are avante garde reflections
on a movie screen never
seen by another human being

What I experience
what I feel
is dream reality;
the real, a waking dream.

A pinch registers pain but it's just
reflexes of the skin,
a sense of being.

Does thinking painful
thoughts yield swollen feelings?

Do the pangs of past remembrance
pulse cryptic in my head
like so many things said
like all the colors turning red
like so many hairs in the bed
like a genius can't be led
alive yet looking dead
a hemophilic looking to be bled

so what hurts is emotional sensation
better not to admit to revelation
the pluses add up to negative equations.

Pray only for spiritual liberation.

<u>SOLID</u>

No pot, no speeed
no need for the negatives
that draw from me
accomplishing prerogatives

Back on a strong cycle
full of iron and input and positives
late to bed, early to rise
makes a man tired by the weekend
spends a man before his time

I've been looking in and measured my works
done for the good of the people
become selfless in my pursuits
now the payoff is coming

THE CHRISTMAS TREE

Blink.....
Blink.....
Blink.....
Blink.....
Went the lights on the tree
That circled in rings
on the limbs in the green
Orange, blue, red, yellow
White, purple and pink
all rowed
Like Bright soldiers
marching circles
to the peak
blink.....
blink.....
blink.....
blink.....

<u>SET IT STRAIGHT</u>

I wish I would have said
more than"goodbye."
I didn't want to leave
anyone crying
So I patted your shoulder
and kissed your rough lips
to travel on another of
my numerous trips
While you rode the corridors
which led to an end

I wish I would have made you
quit, but you'll never end
Your life was your own
though it's hard to realize
that's the way you wanted it
we just never thought you'd
quit living so suddenly, so…

Now you're playing gin with
the angels and I'm drinking
your wine;
so this is why it's so dry
and bitter this time
it's the last we'll have to swallow
us mortal survivors
who prayed by your bedside
to be left with reminders
like wine and stew
and weapons of living
you don't have to fight anymore
we'll do your grieving
Neil, Dad, Papa Bear, Grandpa,
you left a mark that's more
than law
gave us something to look
up to, someone to love
but we'll never be the same
now that you're a dove
you took part of us with you
now we're only whole when
we think of you near us

why did you have to go?
So sad, so separated you
wouldn't like us this way
but we feel your
presence each day
and sometimes we cry
sometimes reminisce
because to us you were so
much larger than life
charisma, presence, your style
and finesse
you let us see you undressed

Look down on us friend
if not with your presence
just guide us to your end
for reunion in heaven.

There once was a drunken Eccentric
Fattened on hors d'oeuvres and beer
Crosseyed and bursting
And clearly the worst in
158 Erie St. Tuesday.

COME HOME INFIDEL

"Inside outside
LEAVE ME ALONE
Inside outside
NOWHERE IS HOME
inside outside
WHERE HAVE I BEEN
OUT OF MY BRAIN...." Quadrophenia

In place of pleasure
comes guilt
It's hard to measure fun
The cost high
the substance strong
Why do I go wrong?

Release means grief
on a rope of twine
Why do I fuck
with this life of mine?

I climb a mountain
to slide belly down
Arrive at the bottom
the same old clown
Abuse, rebuild, abuse, debilitate
come home infidel.

EVERYTHING IS NOTHING

Doing
nothing
does
something
to me.

<u>BUT HOPE 6-9-86</u>

Say goodbye to the brilliant blues,
without them you will lose
all that means anything to your
self esteem, dignity, your seeds.

Depressed from depressants
downed out from uppers
the balance of what's left is
moldy and crusted
Don't be down,
get up, get up, get up
I'm busted and used, my fuse has
turned ashen
Sadness bid welcome to madness
and there's no reason for the cost
I must pay, not my choice, yet
I still play, for
days and days and days.

Let's have a different game for
sameness draws an end to me,
never content with simplicity,
complacency is not in my vocabulary
I am of action and excitement while
my life sits a dry spout
run out of life by my own
needless fears and tears that
won't come I want to
run and run and run
but I'm so tired from running
the ground blurs in front of me
while the past flashes mirages
of what might have been
The heat suffocates while the
chill prickles skin, a flu of
deception and failure that's too long
set in. I must puke my heart out
again and again and again.
There's nothing left.

POOROETRY

www.ingramcontent.com/pod-product-compliance
Lightning Source LLC
Chambersburg PA
CBHW030012040426
42337CB00012BA/753